Dominique the Donkey

~~~~~

the story of
why the donkey
wears a cross

~~~~~

By Cynthia Lane

Illustrations by
Catherine Clough

© 2014 Cynthia Lane

Dedicated with gratitude and respect to

*Karol Jozef Wojtyla,
Blessed Pope John Paul II,
who embodied the spirit of service*

and

*Rev. Father James Fryar, FSSP,
whose encouragement and support
made this mission possible*

iv

Episodes

The Dream	1
The Journey	6
The Arrival	11
The Awakening	15

The Dream

It was Dominique's wildest dream.

Majestic Diamond Peak wore a crown of clouds. It was the highest of the sacred mountains in the Land of the Sands, and Dominique had lived her young life in its protective shadow.

She often looked up to the place where its tip pierced the very blue sky and pondered the secret of the meaning of life that was surely hidden there.

No wild donkey had ever climbed the peak before, and her herd mates shunned her for dreaming of it. They would not stand nose to nose with her, even at night, when it was cold.

So Dominique spent her solitary youth exploring the vast valleys and pleasant pastures and high hills near the mountain. She knew the sheep and the camels and every donkey in her herd by their names and their natures.

And she knew that there was more to know.

It was the Wise Old Donkey who had inspired Dominique's dream.

One day, when she was wondering about the meaning of life, she asked him for help.

"It is time for you to make a Journey of the most important sort," the Wise Old Donkey told her, his brown eyes twinkling. "If you can find your Way to Diamond Peak, your wildest dream will come true."

One morning, not long afterward, before the other donkeys had begun to stir, Dominique's instinct awakened her. It was time to go.

She looked fondly and a little sadly at her herd, and with a soft snort and a robust resolve, she headed toward the highest height.

The early morning sun peeked over the smallest peak,  crept a bit higher, then hid behind a taller one. The glowing globe played hide and seek all morning until it finally broke free of the mountain range to begin its westward roll.

Dominique was thinking about how high Diamond Peak was and what might lie along the Way when she came upon Jerusalem, the village of the desert people. They hung tinkling bells from the necks of their tame donkeys. The sound made her cringe with fear.

Many domesticated donkeys served the desert people, offering their milk for food.

They carried heavy loads for the people, and sometimes carried people, too. They walked in circles around grist mills, grinding meal for the people's bread. Some even gave their lives so the people could make clothing from their hide.

It was hard for Dominique to wish the people well. She watched the tame donkeys at their humble tasks, feeling sorry for them. After all, she was a wild donkey, and she knew there was so much more in store for her on Diamond Peak than the life they lived in the village.

Dominique's instinct was to avoid the people, but at the edge of the village was a well, and Dominique was thirsty, thirstier than she was afraid. She was so busy drinking that she didn't notice Joseph walking up beside her.

Before she realized it, he had lightly taken hold of her mane. Dominique struggled to break free, but Joseph's voice was kind and gentle.

"Would you help me, little donkey?" he asked her.

From behind the well, Mary emerged. She drew near to the donkey, looking at her with grateful eyes.

Dominique's sympathy for the young mother-to-be calmed her wild nature, and she stood still while Joseph helped Mary onto Dominique's back. It was the first time anyone had ridden her, and it would take some getting used to.

"Thank God for you, little donkey," Mary said, relieved that she didn't have to walk to Bethlehem.

As Dominique trudged along in the hot sand, she saw Diamond Peak growing smaller and smaller in the distance.

"The people are leading me away from my dream," she thought to herself. She couldn't have known that the Truth was just the opposite.

The Journey

Dominique listened to the soft sound her steps made in the sand under her hooves. Besides her own breathing and Mary's occasional humming, it was the only sound in the barren wilderness.

She walked as if in a dream. Looking into the vast blanket of sand, her mind grew still and blank, as it was before she had learned anything. She lost awareness of her footsteps, her breathing, her fears, even time itself. She became lost in what she was doing in the present moment, which was the beginning of finding her Way on the Journey.

As the sun began to set, its beams climbed the desert hills, sending pink and peach and lavender light up onto the rocks in a last burst of color before the purple twilight came.

Joseph stopped at the first gate they came to, and knocked. "May we stay here for the night?" he asked. "My wife is so tired, and we have been traveling all day."

"There is no room," the man said. "People are here from everywhere for the census."

Wherever they stopped, the story was the same.

A luminous lone star was rising in the inky black sky, its light making the sand sparkle, when Joseph finally found a stable where they could stay.

He brought Dominique inside and closed the door, and helped Mary off the donkey's back and onto a bed of straw. The sound of the door made Dominique feel trapped, just another domestic farm animal like the sheep and goats in the stable. Dominique thought once again of her dream, to reach Diamond Peak, and settled into a restless night.

When the sun rose over the desert, Dominique awoke and saw Mary, still in her bed of straw, and in the manger beside her, a newborn baby. The young donkey's maternal instinct awakened and drew her to the boy, and she nuzzled Him with her velvety nose.

The baby Jesus reached out to touch her face, and smiled. Dominique had never felt anything like this before, and her instant and overpowering love for Him pushed Diamond Peak from her thoughts, for the moment.

The days went by, as days do, and with each one that passed, Dominique became more at home with Jesus, Mary and Joseph. There were many visitors to the little stable, including three kings carrying precious gifts for the baby.

But one day, Mary climbed onto Dominique's back, and Joseph handed the infant Jesus to her and led the family outside, onto the road.

Dominique wondered where they were going, but she was not worried. She was happy just to be with the family. That night, she made herself into a warm pillow for the baby. Jesus looked happily up at Dominique, and for an instant, Dominique thought she saw something of the Wise Old Donkey in the boy's gentle brown eyes.

During the next morning's walk, they passed Diamond Peak in the distance, but it had been swallowed in clouds, and Dominique did not even notice it.

After a long passage, they arrived home to Nazareth. Mary slid off Dominique's back and touched her forehead to the donkey's forelock.

"Thank you, dear donkey," she said to Dominique. "You can go now."

Go where? Dominique was puzzled.

Joseph removed her blanket. "On your Way, little donkey," he said, as the family went inside. "You have served us well. Enjoy your freedom."

Dominique stood outside the little house for a long while, until she heard Jesus laughing with His mother.

Satisfied, yet sad, she set off halfheartedly in the direction of Diamond Peak.

Days later, she reached the base of the sacred mountain, wearing its hazy halo.

As Dominique contemplated climbing it, she slowly realized there was nothing at the top that she didn't already possess.

How she had wanted to reach that place with everything in her, grasping at its promise to reveal the meaning of life.

And how mysterious that her wildest dream had come true by letting it go for the benefit of someone else.

The Arrival

The years passed as Dominique happily continued serving people.

For a time, she worked for a rich Samaritan, who once found a wounded man on the side of the road to Jericho. Though others ignored him, the Samaritan treated his wounds and had Dominique carry him to the safety of an inn.

She did many such deeds, but there was one special task she wanted to complete before she reached the end of her journey – to teach her wild herd mates what she had learned.

As she made her way back to the valley below Diamond Peak, where she had spent her youth, the familiar bells of her domesticated relations tinkled in the nearby village. She no longer cringed at the sound.

She saw her wild herd peacefully speckling the landscape in the foothills, and trotted over, beginning to recognize their faces.

But they didn't recognize her.

Dominique was no longer the little brown donkey they had known. She had turned golden from head to hoof.

One of the herd walked slowly toward her, stopped, and bowed his gray head.

It was the Wise Old Donkey, who had pointed the Way. He stepped aside for Dominique to pass.

As the days and months went by, Dominique again became part of her wild herd. She found a mate, and they had a colt, which she named Dominic, meaning, "belonging to the Lord." She taught him about her Journey, and what he could learn about the meaning of life from the service of their domesticated relations.

When he was of age, Dominic decided he would join the tame donkeys in the town and try to be of service. His mother was very proud, but tears came to her eyes as he trotted away toward Jerusalem.

One day, not long afterward, a crowd gathered at the town gate, attracting Dominique's attention.

There was no mistaking Him, even so many years later; His gentle, brown eyes, the laugh she remembered so well.

Dominique wanted to gallop to Him, but something stopped her.

Just inside the gate, tied to a post, was her son, Dominic, on the verge of fulfilling his destiny.

Suddenly, a man took hold of Dominic.

"Master, here!" Peter said to Him. "The King of Kings should not walk into Jerusalem, but ride!"

Jesus looked into the colt's eyes and smiled, climbing onto his back.

Dominic carried Him as gingerly as a vase of precious water in the desert, the living repository of all that is sacred.

He walked on, not noticing that the crowd was pressing in, or that the palm leaves under his hooves were sharp, or that the crowd was shouting "Hosanna!"

Just as his mother had taught him, He had lost himself in service to Jesus, as she had done so many years ago, when she had first begun to find her Way on the Journey.

When Jesus slid off Dominic's back, He pressed His forehead to the donkey's forelock to thank him, just as His mother had done to Dominic's mother when they parted.

The Awakening

Dominic followed Jesus closely every day, until one Friday, when he could not get near Him to help with the heavy wooden cross He carried down the street, through the village gate and up the hill of Calvary.

As Dominic reached the foot of the hill, he saw his mother approaching from her wild herd outside the town.

They watched together in bewilderment as Jesus was crucified, knowing that all the burdens that they and their domesticated relations had carried and all the sacrifices they had made for people were nothing compared to this mysterious kind of service to others.

As Mary gazed at her Son through her tears, Dominic looked to his own mother for answers, which she was just beginning to understand herself.

Jesus was not just the end of her Journey, He was the Way.

He was not just her wildest dream coming true, He was the Truth.

He was not just the meaning of life, He was Life itself.

As the afternoon sun rolled across the sky, the cross cast a fleeting shadow across Dominique's back, which had borne Mary safely to Bethlehem.

Then it passed across Dominic's back, which had carried Jesus gloriously into Jerusalem.

And to this day, that shadow is still seen on the backs of donkeys, a reminder of young Dominic and his mother, who once dreamed of finding the meaning of life at the top of a peak, only to awaken and find it at the foot of a hill.

Artist Catherine Clough is a home-schooled high schooler who sings with the Ala Prexque schola and the Saint Philomena Children's Choir at Christ the King Catholic Church in Sarasota, Florida. Her love of drawing is rivaled only by her love of animals and singing. She relies on her Catholic faith for inspiration and strength.

Made in the USA
Lexington, KY
03 November 2015